WILLIAM MORRIS

DISCOVERING ART

The Life, Times and Work of the World's Greatest Artists

WILLIAM MORRIS

N. M. WELLS

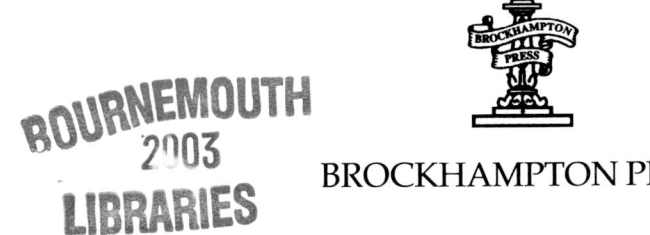

BROCKHAMPTON PRESS

This book is dedicated to Carey, for her patient encouragement, and to Douglas, for living.

Author's note:
All quotes are taken from Morris's writings, lectures and letters, unless otherwise stated.

First published in Great Britain by Brockhampton Press,
a member of the Caxton Publishing Group,
20 Bloomsbury Street, London WC1B 3JH

ISBN 1 84186 0913

Produced by Flame Tree Publishing,
The Long House, Antrobus Road, Chiswick, London W4 5HY
for Brockhampton Press.
A Wells/McCreeth/Sullivan Production

Pictures printed courtesy of the Visual Arts Library, London, the Trustees of the V&A, London and Edimedia, Paris.

Printed and bound by Oriental Press, Dubai

CONTENTS

Portrait of William Morris (William Morris Gallery, London). Taken in his middle years, this contemporary photograph depicts a strong face with a steady, confident stare. There are signs of the endless restless searching which characterized the breadth of his work.

CHRONOLOGY

1834	Born at Elm House, Walthamstow, Essex.
1848-51	Marlborough School.
1853-5	Exeter College, Oxford.
1854	Formative trip to Belgium and Northern France.
1855-6	Launched *Oxford and Cambridge Magazine*.
1856	Articled to G.E. Smith, architect.
1857	Painted frescoes in Oxford Union.
1858	Published *The Defence of Guenevere and Other Poems*.
1859	Married Jane Burden.
	Founded Morris & Co.
1861	First daughter, Jenny, born.
1862	May Morris born.
1865	Moved to Queen Square, Bloomsbury, London.
1867	*The Life and Death of Jason* published.
	Morris & Co. decorated Green Dining Room, V&A Museum, London.
1868-70	*The Earthly Paradise* published.
1872	First wallpaper design *Larkspur*.
	Love is Enough published.
1873	Visited Iceland and Italy.
1876	Appointed Examiner at School of Art, South Kensington, London.
	Opened showroom in Oxford Street.
1877	Wrote manifesto *To the Working-men of England*.
	Formed The Society for the Protection of Ancient Buildings.
	First lecture, on The Lesser Arts, the decorative arts.
1881	Morris & Co. works moved to Merton Abbey, Surrey.
1882	Volume of Lectures published, *Hopes and Fears for Art*
	Rossetti died.
1883	Designed *Strawberry Thief*.
	Joined Democratic Federation, later the Social Democratic Federation (SDF).
1884	Helped found Socialist League.
	Foundation of Art Workers Guild.
1885	Arrested at a trial of Socialists, discharged.
1886	*A Dream of John Bull* appeared in *Commonweal*.
1887	Bloody Sunday 13 November.
	Foundation of the Arts and Crafts Exhibition Society.
1888	Published *A Dream of John Bull* in book form.
	Published the prose romance *House of the Wolfungs*.
1890	Published *News from Nowhere* in instalments.
	Left Socialist League, formed Hammersmith Socialist Society.
	Founded Kelmscott Press.
1891	Published *News from Nowhere* and *Poems by the Way*.
1893	Helped draft Manifesto of English Socialists.
1895	Published translation of *Beowulf*.
1896	Published Kelmscott edition of Chaucer.
	3 October, died and buried at Kelmscott.

Iris and Bird, c. 1880s. Sometimes referred to simply as *Iris*, this wallpaper design has proved to be one of Morris's most enduring patterns. It can be found today reproduced on the cover of many books and diaries, and indeed is still available as a wallpaper.

Introduction

Rebellion

The works of William Morris pulsate with energy, passion and inventiveness. His appeal, still strong today through the medium of his designs for wallpapers and fabrics, derives from the breadth of his achievements, a concern for his fellow man and the powerfully sympathetic response to nature which fed the swirling patterns of his decorative designs.

Overleaf:
Acanthus, 1880 (Victoria & Albert Museum, London). This is one of Morris's most beautiful designs, an embroidered wall hanging. The layers of pattern within pattern lead the viewer to follow each line of leaf and flower until a new line is discovered, leading again to another strand, another lyrical reflection of the natural world.

Poet, painter, designer, typographer, polemicist, manufacturer and Socialist, Morris leapt from one enthusiasm to another, living his life with a restless energy that led him constantly to seek and solve new challenges. At his core was the commitment to a basic philosophy that good design came from a good society. He was a warm, generous man prone to enraged frustrations, a sensitive man who could be brutal in his constant grip on quality. His mastery over one craft after another ensured his absolute dominance in the field of the decorative arts where he is assured of his position as the greatest British pattern designer.

His contemporaries regarded him with a mixture of reverence and affection. The designer and teacher Lethaby, a prodigious talent himself, declared that Morris was the '...greatest pattern designer we have had or ever can have, for a man of scale will not again be working in the minor arts'. W.B. Yeats, in *Autobiographies* 1955, said that 'If some angel offered me the choice, I would rather live his life, poetry and all rather than my own or any other man's.' Bernard Shaw wrote that Morris was 'great not only among little men but among great ones'.

These observations, from men of very different disciplines reveal Morris's strengths. To all appearances the scale of his interests and achievements can be daunting if taken methodically, one at a time. To do so would undermine the essential diversity and range of a man whose doctor reported that the cause of death was 'simply being William Morris, and having done more work than most ten men'. He toiled with a rumbustuous joy that drove his broad creative energies hard. To many he seemed like a Renaissance man, which is ironic because he detested the period and all it stood for, and yet he was straightforward in his motivations, above all a designer, signing himself as such when he joined the Democratic Federation in 1883. This essentially simple vocation informed his thinking and absorbed his attention: for Morris there was a strong moral association between the artist and his work. He believed that true artists were people who could express themselves completely through the material they worked with, benefiting from the full value of their labours. He did not, however, fully express himself in any one activity, settling instead for a complex vortex of crafts, arts, literature and politics as though no single medium could contain the passionate committed turmoil of his imagination.

It is ironic that today the name William Morris is linked with the notion of Victorian design. This would have enraged Morris. His philosophies on the rightness of art, the value of human endeavour and the corrupting nature of manufacturing for profit runs in direct opposition to Victorian society. The artifice, indulgence and shoddy workmanship represented by industrial advances were anathema to him. He preferred sentiment to sentimentality, natural simplicity to artificial

profusion. Such tensions gave rise to much of his greatest work, ranging from the beauty of the Kelmscott edition of Chaucer's *Canterbury Tales*, the burgeoning tendrils of the wallpaper design *Honeysuckle* and the strident honesty of his lectures on art and democracy in the 1880s.

Morris fulminated against the dehumanizing industrialization which fuelled the economy of the British Empire. He did not object to the machines themselves but their use by some to produce profits through the exploitation of others. This was part of an holistic world view which saw art as a litmus test for the health of the nation. 'Unless people care about carrying on their business without making the world hideous, how can they care about art?' he declared. The production of shoddy goods for the express purpose of making only profit led

Peacock and Dragon, 1878 (Private Collection). Morris's fabrics became highly fashionable from the mid-1870s. In this woven wool hanging, dramatic tension within the design between the peacock and the dragon seems to bring the pattern to life even though it is highly formalized. The use of the dragon motif, with its sharp, positive curves shows the heavy influence of the Middle and Far East, which resulted from the expanding trade between countries of the British Empire.

Design for embroidered panel, undated (Victoria & Albert Museum, London). This half-painted design shows how Morris, in common with his contemporaries, worked out his designs in solid painted colours before committing them to the final material. The panel establishes the colours, the contrasts, the relative weights of each line, showing the craftsman who would produce the final item exactly how it should appear.

to a decline in the moral standing of those who were forced to produce them. Only by making, for instance, furniture, honestly with a true joy in the craftsmanship and a share in the benefits in making it, could people become true to themselves.

Morris, like many of the thinkers and artists of the day, looked back to the pre-industrial Middle Ages where a sense of natural order prevailed, where there was respect for the countryside and an understanding of the value in a craftsman's work. Like the poetry of Tennyson, the music of Wagner and the paintings of Millais, Morris sought to express his vision of the world through an ideal medieval landscape, turning, initially, from the squalor of the nineteenth century to an escape into romance, mythology and chivalry. Later, equipped with the experiences of his exceptional life he sought to change the world he lived in rather than seek a temporary escape from it. He harnessed the lessons of the past into a unified vision of society where art was intrinsic to everyday life. This was a search for a better life through constructive criticism, positive action and by example.

Morris saw no difference between the maker and the thinker, the artist and the politician, because he was all of these things himself and he understood that relative values were false, that the skills of one contributor to society such as a thinker like Thomas Carlyle or John Ruskin were no greater than those human skills of making a chair or a painting. He rarely compromised on his strong sense of vision, which included the requirement to think and feel through the raw materials that were used, 'Never forget the material you are working with, and always try to use it for what it can do best.' This came partly from a desire to reflect the flowing lines and rough fluidity of the natural world. He drew a precise and lyrical pleasure from the whole process of designing his patterns, ranging from the research of natural and historical references to the physical mixing of the colour for the cloth.

William Morris was a rare and genuine force of cultural change. Raymond Williams in his critical analysis, *Culture and Society 1780-1950*, regarded him as a central figure in the development of modern culture. Morris was an entrepreneur of unusual creativity, surrounding himself with a cauldron of talented people, Edward Burne-Jones, Dante Gabriel Rossetti, Ford Madox Brown, Philip Webb and Arthur Mackmurdo, who were all drawn to and sympathetic with his rebellion against Victorian values. The clarity and honesty of his approach enabled these men and many others to define their own expression of revolt against the Age and turn this to a more worthy future.

The society they strove against, however, was a powerful enemy.

The Victorian Age

Morris lived during a commercial and industrial explosion. By the mid-nineteenth century Britain, through its Empire, was the most powerful nation in the World. By conquering countries and establishing sovereignty over peoples in Africa, Asia and India, exotic materials came flooding back to the mother country for the first time. The colonies became new markets for goods produced in Britain, often using material originating in the colonies themselves. Society grew increasingly prosperous as Britain became the 'workshop of the world'. With the confidence that such success brings, new enterprises and innovations heralded a rapidly changing life for the people of Britain. An enhanced work ethic showed people that endeavour could bring high reward, with wealthy businessmen making their fortunes out of manufacturing. The Industrial Revolution was fuelled by the new railway network connecting towns and factories, the electric telegraph improving communication and a booming trade with the colonies for merchant shipping. With mechanization came mass production as work formerly carried out by hand was accelerated by steam and steel. Wide availability brought cheaper prices and wider

Strawberry Thief, **1883.** A simple, powerful repeating-pattern wallpaper, *Strawberry Thief* is perhaps the most widely recognized of Morris's designs and represents one of his most vibrant, accessible creations, a stylized, gently wry celebration of nature at play.

choice. It seemed as though the whole world was within reach, with capitalism bringing the benefits of world peace and prosperity.

The tangibility of progress and profit was a vital part of the excitement and energy in Victorian society and it was epitomized by the Great Exhibition of 1851. The Exhibition building itself boasted ostentatiously of its newness. It displayed objects, furnishings, art and commercial goods from the whole British Empire. Forty-three thousand people visited it daily with over six million people attending in total. Queen Victoria revelled in this magnificent shrine to her age and its achievements.

However, to William Morris, even as a sixteen-year-old visitor with his mother, the Great Exhibition was a vulgar abomination and he strove for the rest of his life to undermine its effect. For all its opulence, its offer of choice, prosperity and influence there was something terrible and rotten at its core. The raw power of progress flattered to deceive, with mass production resulting in poor quality, quickly made goods and the means of production consigning a large part of society to an existence of grinding misery.

For Morris there were two strands to his rejection of these values. The first was at the purely aesthetic level where the coarse, shoddy workmanship with its surface illusion of beauty existed only to sell itself and to be placed as an object of admiration in its own right: the ornate chairs, the overabundant vases and carpets, the veneered tables appealed to the sensibilities at the level of the lowest common denominator. It looked pretty, it invited sentimental nostalgia, a pseudo-romantic past was exploited to deliver a spurious sense of authenticity. In Morris's view this cynical illusion of beauty, designed to appeal to a gullible and unsophisticated consumer, masked a lack of both integrity and quality.

The second strand is inextricably linked with the first. Morris rebelled at the cost of producing such dazzling, ostentatious artifice. He counted this cost both in terms of the human and natural worlds, for the creeping horror of smoking, bellowing factories on the lush green dales and English hedgerows had its parallels in the increasing misery of the labouring classes whose lives were also corrupted by the creeping, smoking factories. The contributions of these people to Britain's new found wealth was undermined by the lack of actual skills required to run the machines.

Their work became a commodity of low value where once it had been something to be proud of. For Morris, the Industrial Revolution had disenfranchised a section of society which had formerly created its own livelihood and on which the sense of self-worth and moral strength of craftsman skills, depended. This response to mechanized progress developed into a philosophy of life, art and society as unified and interrelated forces. Art in all its forms, from fine oil paintings to crafted furniture and tapestries, was a reflection of the society which produced it. If that society made superficially pretty but shoddy art by using the people who made it, then discarding them for profit, then the art itself degraded the makers, the craftsmen and, by extension, society itself. To Morris this was a moral issue and art could not be separated from it.

Later he would lecture on art which must have an everyday relevance, a connection with the environment in which it existed. 'Have nothing about you which is not useful,' he said and the decorative and domestic arts in which he specialized were deliberate expressions of his beliefs. Such notions had gained currency for the first time in the late eighteenth century with Samuel Taylor Coleridge and Thomas Carlyle being early advocates, but the main critic and first major influence on Morris's thought was Ruskin who developed them into a devastating intellectual critique of contemporary society.

It is important to note the contradictory forces within Victorian society, the flamboyant dash for progress on the one hand, the restraining hand of moral rectitude on the other. Ruskin challenged this directly in his celebrated definition of beauty which declared two clear notions, of 'vital beauty' and 'typical beauty'. The latter refers to art, 'the external quality of body ... which, whether it occurs in a stone, flower, beast or man, is absolutely identical; which ... may be shown to be in some sort typical of divine attribute.' 'Vital beauty' is 'the appearance of felicitous fulfilment of function in living things, more especially of the joyful and right exertion of perfect life in man.' It was this 'vital beauty' which the grotesque capitalistic values of the Victorian age failed to deliver. Ruskin declared that 'The art of any country is the exponent of its social and political values.' There is a sense of fairness and equality in these words, a refreshing decency which found a powerful echo in the viscera of William Morris and the painters of the Pre-Raphaelite Brotherhood whose own artistic rebellion Ruskin was to advocate and defend so vigorously. For Morris, Ruskin was his own Great Exhibition, epitomizing the instincts and values of his convictions. Later Morris moved to a more direct, critical analysis of society, through Marx and early revolutionary Socialism but his response was always characterized by a forthright honesty, in contrast to the supercilious elitism of some of his artistic contemporaries.

Woodland Weeds (Victoria & Albert Museum, London). By the early 1880s Morris's designs were established as the most pre-eminent and challenging of his generation. This example shows Morris combining the fluid lines of nature with the rigid two-dimensional demands of wallpaper patterns.

CHAPTER 1

Dreams and Realities

A lively sense of rebelliousness characterized the young William Morris; his response to the complacent materialism of the Victorian age was typical of the questioning and seeking which drove him for the rest of his life.

Overleaf:
Section from the fireplace mantel, by Morris, Rossetti, Madox Brown, Burne-Jones, 1862-4 (Queens College Hall, Cambridge). The commission to decorate the College Hall was a major collaborative work by the four artists with tiles, wallpapers and panels all harnessed to convey a gorgeous richness and depth.

Morris was born on 24 March 1834 at Elm House, in Clay Hill, Walthamstow to the north-east of London. At that time it was a languorous Essex village with the sweeping majesty of Epping Forest to the north side and the lush undulations of the Lea Valley to the south. Meadows and farmlands stretched into the distance where the River Thames was marked by the gently drifting sails of wherries. It was a wild bowl of natural life, a living watercolour painting which lay dreamily at the heart of Morris's life, always an inspiration for his work and repose, an image of Eden for his poetry, prose and decorative designs.

He was born into a family whose wealth came from the money his father had speculated in a copper mine. The commercial success of the venture brought considerable freedom and opportunity to Morris, the contradictions of which he came to appreciate later in life when he campaigned on behalf of the working man. He was an intelligent young boy, always reading but restlessly turning from one book or one interest to another. He readily absorbed information and literature and it is said that he had read all of Walter Scott's *Waverley* novels by the age of seven. He was boisterous and given to fits of temper, but read and wrote an endless stream of chivalric romances and fairy stories. His obsessions with knights and fair ladies, elves and fairies provide an early indication of his more romantic preoccupations.

He was sent to the public school Marlborough in 1848 where, he often declared, he 'learnt nothing at all' apart from his own extra-curricular explorations. He spent hours in the Wiltshire countryside studying and delighting in old ruins and churches, in Stonehenge and Avebury. It was a crucial period for him where the freedom to explore was a powerful and instructive force.

However, it was Oxford University that allowed him to develop his intellectual and artistic sensibilities.

Oxford and the Brotherhood

Morris went up to Exeter College, Oxford, in 1853 to study Literature and the Classics. It was in the 'vision of grey roofed houses, a long street and the sound of many bells' that he met the full force of medievalism and numerous friends, indulged in the interests and engaged in the arguments which founded many of the beliefs and passions of his life. He formed a life-long friendship with Edward Burne-Jones, met his future wife Jane Burden and encountered his emotional nemesis Dante Gabriel Rossetti. Here also while in the thrall of John Ruskin he fell in love with illuminated manuscripts and developed as a poet.

From the complex weave of influences during this time a number of important threads can be drawn out. Morris spent a great deal

April Love, Hughes, 1855 (Tate Gallery, London). Morris was entranced by this painting when he first saw it at the Royal Academy exhibition in 1855. With its subtle, broody, wistful evocation of early love it epitomized the attraction of the Pre-Raphaelites for him and he asked Burne-Jones to buy it on his behalf.

Caricature of Morris presenting engagement ring to Jane Burden, Rossetti, 1859 (Birmingham City Museum and Art Gallery). Rossetti and Burne-Jones drew a great many caricatures of Morris, although this is an uncharacteristically affectionate portrait by the man who became obsessed with Burden and whose later caricatures became increasingly ascerbic.

La Belle Iseult, 1858 (Tate Gallery, London). Morris's only surviving painting, the slightly wooden figure is modelled on his then fiancé, and later wife, Jane Burden. On the edge of the canvas he wrote, 'I love you but I cannot paint you' placing an unfortunate emphasis on the central character because the background detail is highly detailed and ornate. Both Rossetti and Ford Madox Brown worked on the painting to improve it in later years.

of time in the Bodleian Library, the home of the best collections of medieval illuminated manuscripts. From this he derived a deeper passion for what he saw as the sense of natural human order, the decorous expression of man and environment in a complementary existence. The physical presence of the manuscripts also made a major impact. Their beautiful, gilded decorative borders and gorgeous dropped, illustrated capitals impressed him with their beauty and their unity of purpose. They were beautiful in their own right but they also expressed the manifest contentment of the monks who decorated them. The delicacy and refinement of each curve and sweep of colour were a reflection of the subject being illustrated and acts of worship in themselves. This unified sense of subject matter and technique had a profound effect on Morris's understanding about the satisfactions of art and craftsmanship. The need for work to be a pleasure in its own right rather than a duty or curse was central to his philosophy of life and later influenced his burgeoning political thought.

The lingering shadow of Victorian artificial gaudiness, and its apogee, the Great Exhibition, contrasted deeply with the illuminated manuscripts which Morris now spent hours studying. He found echoes of their appeal in the writings and lectures of Carlyle and Ruskin which revealed the significance of medieval approach and which explained to Morris why he found their artifice so compelling. Carlyle in his *Sign of the Times* had said, 'Men are grown mechanical in head and in heart, as well as in hand. They have lost faith in individual endeavour, and in natural force of any kind.' Carlyle's appeal for social responsibility from those who drove the commercial machine, was taken up in the social commentary and art criticism of Ruskin. For him the rampant triumph of industrial profit and the consequential degradation of the craftsman demonstrated a massive decline in moral standards. The state of a nation's art reflected the state of its moral health. Art should not be simply a thing of pleasure for those who could afford it but an integral part of the artist himself and the work produced. One of his most penetrating essays was 'On the Nature of the Gothic', from *The Stones of Venice*, where he questioned the validity of commercial success and the rightness of celebrating a success which generated so much human misery.

Examine again all those accurate mouldings, and perfect polishings, and unerring adjustments of the seasoned wood and tempered steel. Many a time you have exulted over them, and thought how great England was, because her slightest work was done so thoroughly. Alas! if read rightly, these perfectnesses are signs of a slavery in our England a thousand times more bitter and more

Jane Morris, Rossetti, 1860 (Private Collection). An early drawing in red chalk of William Morris's wife, two years after their marriage. Rossetti conveys a wistful coolness within the soft tender lines of the chalk.

degrading than that of the scourged African or helot Greek ... sent like fuel to feed the factory smoke.

John Ruskin, *'The Nature of the Gothic'*

Ruskin called for a return to the morality inherent in Gothic architecture which recognized the value in all work done by all men in any project. The nave of Canterbury Cathedral with its lofty reverence and hidden gargoyles is typical of a form of worship which, like the illuminated manuscripts in the Bodleian, was integral to the method of building a religious monument. The pride in the work was the worship and the reward. How different this was from the concerns of industrial Victorian success.

Ruskin's painful analysis was heard by a group of like-minded young men, who called themselves the Brotherhood. It included Morris, Charles Faulkner (a mathematician), R.W. Dixon (a minor religious poet in later life), William Fulford, Cormell Price (later a headmaster), and Edward Burne-Jones. They dedicated themselves to 'a Crusade and Holy Warfare against the age'. Their common interest combined a rebellion against the crass commercialism and materialism of industrial progress with an intense kinship for the Anglo-Catholic preoccupations of the time, represented by the rallying calls of Cardinal Newman. Indeed many of their company, Morris included, expected to become clergymen. Ruskin's *The Nature of the Gothic* was required reading for them all but together they discovered Tennyson, Mallory's *Mort d'Arthur*, Shelley, Keats and Shakespeare, and held readings at which Morris also began to read his own poetry. *The Willow and the Red Cliff* was one of the first poems he exposed at such events and although it is rather awkward, it did demonstrate that he could turn effective poetic phrases with some ease. Morris impressed his contemporaries with his optimistic vitality, his sense of wonder and, as Dixon observed: 'How decisive he was, how accurate, without any effort or formality: what extraordinary power of observation lay at the base of many of his casual and incidental remarks, and how many things he knew that were quite out of our way.'

The St George Cabinet, designed by Philip Webb, 1861 (Victoria & Albert Museum, London). The panels, decorated by Morris and his colleagues are remarkably fine paintings, executed with a genuine affinity for the subject of St George and the chivalric values of his legend.

The Brotherhood's affinity with Ruskin significantly enhanced Morris's instinctive sympathy for the medieval. Morris revelled in his mentor's celebration of Gothic cathedrals and the living, crafted work

Topsy and Ned Jones Settled on the Settle at Red Lion Square, Max Beerbohm, 1916 (Tate Gallery, London). Beerbohm's ironic wash drawing shows William Morris and Edward Burne-Jones sitting on the giant settle designed by Morris and decorated by both of them. They are surrounded by the bare boards of their early London existence, the production of their own settle being a grand monument to their rebellion against the shoddy workmanship of the day. Topsy and Ned were affectionate nicknames used by their friends.

Opposite:
The Brachet Licking Sir Tristam, 1861 (Harden Grange, West Yorkshire Near Bingley). The early 1860s saw Morris & Co. undertake a large number of stained glass projects, inspired by biblical, mythological and classical sources.

in the pillars, the scrollwork and gargoyles. He found a model of medievalism which moved him beyond his early readings of the romances of Walter Scott and encompassed the infant joy of the gardens in Walthamstow and Epping with their natural, flowing lines, the vigorous expression of beauty in the birds, the leaves, the rolling landscape.

In 1855 Morris came of age and was granted a considerable annuity of nine hundred pounds a year. It enabled him to travel with Burne-Jones to Belgium and Northern France. What began as a walking holiday became a turning point in their lives because the two friends encountered the spiralling majesty of the great European cathedrals of Rouen, Chartres, Amiens and Beauvais. They sauntered through beautiful French countryside with 'blue cornflowers and red poppies, growing together with the corn round the roots of the fruit trees, in their shadows, and sweeping up to the brows of the long low hills till they reached the sky, changing sometimes into long fields of vines, or delicate, lush green forage'. This transcendent beauty echoed with his response to the soaring Gothic cathedrals. The land and the Gothic architecture of Northern France were the living embodiments of a past which valued man as part of nature. The magnitude and imposition of the cathedrals provided a direct connection with the past, gently ageing as part of the natural landscape.

During these travels and while studying in Oxford, surrounded by the living splendour of the University buildings, Morris began to

How Sir Tristram slew a giant who would have slain King Mark and how King Mark not know[n]
[h]im brought him to Tintagel, and how he got his wit again and how Isoude knew him again
[c]ause of the brachet which Tristram had given her which leaped upon him and licked h[im]

Honeymoon of King Rene of Anjou, J.P. Seddon, 1862 (Victoria & Albert Museum, London). Morris, Rossetti, Madox Brown and Burne-Jones painted the panels on this oak cabinet designed by J.P. Seddon. It is typical of Morris & Co.'s early work, where almost every inch of surface area was crowded with overt craftsmanship.

Opposite:
The fireplace mantel, by Morris, Rossetti, Madox Brown and Burne-Jones, 1862-4 (Queens College Hall, Cambridge). The scrolling, the motifs and the figures are modelled on the medieval and Gothic subjects which inspired the friends and which provided the inspiration for much of the early work of Morris & Co.

see that architecture was a monument to human value. Its intense immediacy, intimacy and tangibility could be embraced by all who lived with a building, who walked through and around it and, by doing so, celebrated its existence as part of their lives. It was vital therefore that buildings should not be so polished and honed as to be artificial, that the materials used should reflect their origins so that they retained their natural integrity. It was impossible, too, to separate the maker from the made, the finished object from the original material. Morris and the others of the Brotherhood rejected the popular desire to create a uniformity which could easily and quickly be reproduced on a mass scale.

This industrial malaise extended to the methods of restoring old buildings, the process of which had destroyed churches or old buildings which had grown organically according to the needs of the owners or the community, adding a Norman nave to a Saxon fount, or a Victorian pew to an ancient chapel. At Mont St Michel in France for example Morris and his companions were appalled at the restoration work which attempted to return the cathedral to a perceived original form. In later years this reaction was to fuel the campaigning zeal of his Anti-Scrape, The Society for the Preservation of Ancient Buildings. In Belgium and at the Musée de Cluny in Paris the travellers had

Night: Angel Holding Waning Moon, 1864 (Museum of Fine Art, Houston). A watercolour, pencil and collage sketch for a tile on the fireplace mantel in Queens College Hall. The colours softened for the final version but the form remained as originally envisaged.

encountered paintings by the medieval masters Van Eyck and Memlink whose work betrayed their conscious use of natural textures, colours and pigments. The qualities of the natural materials were incorporated into the overall effect of the work of art, whether it was in the form of a painting, a building or a piece of furniture. Morris and Burne-Jones had also discovered in Paris a travelling exhibition of paintings by the early Pre-Raphaelites, including Rossetti, at the Louvre.

On their return they decided to abandon their previous intentions to enter the church. Morris, convinced that art, writing and poetry could not sufficiently embrace the past, opted for architecture. Burne-Jones, already heavily impressed by Rossetti's work in Oxford took painting as his occupation.

In 1885 Morris and his associates started the *Oxford and Cambridge Magazine* which allowed members of the Brotherhood to publish their writings. He contributed one-third of his new annual income to the project, and became the editor and proprietor. Together the Brotherhood decided to publish social articles, prose romances and poetry which reflected the concerns of the Group: the contrast of their Victorian age with an imagined medieval one which was founded on respect, moral leadership and a true sense of a morally ordered society. In such a society a man could truly fulfil himself through his work. Morris declared that 'it would be well of all if us were good handicraftsmen in some kind, and the dishonour of manual labour done away with altogether.' In his own writing he was content to portray 'the embodiment of dreams in one form or other' following romantic convention with straightforward depictions of good and evil, truth and beauty. The poem, *In Praise of My Lady*, is a praise of ideal womanhood containing no sense of sensuous physical presence. His attitude to women, determined by the traditional values of the time but also the idealized images of women in his beloved medieval inspirations, were of unsullied, unsensual beings.

> *Her Great eyes, standing far apart,*
> *Draw up some memory from her heart,*
> *And gaze out mournfully;*
> – Beata mea Domina! –
>
> *So beautiful and kind they are,*
> *But most times looking out afar,*
> *Waiting for something, not for me*
> – Beata mea Domina! –
> In Praise of My Lady, *1857*

This directly contrasted with the sensual work of the more mature, charismatic Rossetti by whom Morris and his set were increasingly overwhelmed. Indeed, Morris's first published collection of verse, *The Defence of Guenevere* was dedicated to Rossetti and included several poems inspired by his paintings.

The Lure of Rossetti

Morris left Oxford to be articled to the architect G.E. Smith in 1856. J.W. Mackail, Morris's first biographer, readily identified the significance of this move, writing that to be an architect was to be '... connected at a thousand points with all other specific arts which administered to it out of a thousand sources, it was itself the tangible expression of all the order, the comeliness, the sweetness, nay even the mystery, the law, which sustains man's work and makes human life what it is'. Unfortunately, within nine months he had wearied of the process of training to become an architect.

At G.E. Smith's he met Philip Webb, who became a lifelong friend and colleague. He recalled of those early months that Morris would repeatedly hit his forehead in frustration and that 'He was out of place in an office.' The theory of architecture was too remote for Morris, he possessed strong ideas of his own, high standards and an intolerance of people who could or would not do what he wanted them to do. Handing over designs to another to manufacture was increasingly frustrating to him at a time when he was falling to the allure of Rossetti. Burne-Jones had already apprenticed to this stylish, handsome, celebrated painter and November 1856 Morris and Burne-Jones found premises together in Red Lion Square in London where they joined the melting pot of the later Pre-Raphaelites.

John Everett Millais's *Autumn Leaves* (1854), William Holman Hunt's *Scapegoat* (1854) and Arthur Hughes' *April Love* (1855) are regarded as some of the finest examples of Pre-Raphaelite art. Morris had seen and fallen in love particularly with the tearful melancholy of Hughes' masterpiece and it pressed him further into the glittering influence of Rossetti and the movement which specifically rejected the 'clear and tasteless poison of the art of Raphael'. They were championed by John Ruskin, who was painted by them, as saviours of art against the tyranny of artificiality. They tried to bring truth and nature together, using literary allusion and a celebrated, passionate sense of religion. Their subjects although medieval were not treated as living legends, but as part of the landscape which surrounded them. The mighty heroes of Mallory's *Mort d'Arthur* and classical mythology were painted as reflections of the natural world, not as conquerors or elevated from it. The high Renaissance traditions of Raphael and Tintoretto were circumnavigated for a more emblematic approach to man in his world. In method as well as subject matter the Pre-Raphaelites rebelled against

Day: Angel Holding Sun, 1864 (Museum of Fine Art, Houston). The companion piece to *Night*, placed together in the fireplace mantel, above the figures representing each season.

their predecessors. Instead of employing thick, dark strokes they used a wet, white surface upon which thousands of meticulous, fine strokes were built up in luminous colours.

Rossetti was a poet as well as painter but for him Keats had already scaled the heights and explored high excellence. He said, 'If a man has any poetry in him he should paint, for it has all been said and written, and they have scarcely begun to paint it.' Painting was the highest form of art, engaging every sense, relying extensively on both a visceral and intellectual response from the viewer, a continuing dialogue between the painter, his subject and the viewer.

Rossetti became, in Burne-Jones's words, 'the planet around which we all revolved' and was the instrument of a major venture in 1857. He was commissioned to decorate the gallery of the new debating hall at the Oxford Union. Morris, Burne-Jones, Arthur Hughes and Rossetti set about painting ten panels, scenes from *Mort d'Arthur*. Morris's contribution was uncomfortably prophetic, choosing 'How Sir Palomydes loved La Belle Iseult with an exceeding great love, and how she loved him not again, but rather Sir Tristram.' Significantly, Morris also decorated the ceiling with sensuous, climbing tendrils, an imaginative repeated pattern which was to mark the beginning of his original approach to decorative detail. The decorators clearly had a great deal of fun with Morris commissioning the manufacture of real armour for use as references and in which they clattered around and laughed. Perhaps too much fun was had by all because their apparent lack of knowledge of fresco work led to their painted panels fading almost completely within a single year. The paint had been applied on to damp plaster without proper preparation.

Unable to buy the quality of goods they required because of the standard of mass-produced furniture, Burne-Jones and Morris made their first attempts at making their own. This gave Morris some satisfaction because his painting was not going well. His awkwardness with figures held him back and gave him the same frustrations he experienced as an apprentice to G.E. Smith.

In 1857 he met Jane Burden and competed with his illustrious friend and sometime mentor, Rossetti, for her attentions. She was the daughter of a local ostler and had first been noticed by Burne-Jones and Rossetti. They were drawn to her dark hair, alluring eyes and luxuriant hair: she was the very antithesis of the classic English rose and they persuaded her parents to allow her to sit for them, modelling for Guinevere in *Lancelot in the Queen's Chamber* and the Princess in *The Wedding of St George*. Morris also painted her, as Iseult in *Iseult on the Ship* and, with Rossetti, fell in love with their mutual artistic muse. She was an acknowledged beauty of the time and became the inspiration of the Pre-Raphaelite movement. She was the motivating force behind much of Rossetti's later poetry, the model of many of his paintings,

Blanzifiore (Snowdrops), Rossetti, 1873 (Private Collection). Jane Burden continued to be Rossetti's muse for the rest of his life. The delicate curves of the snowdrops are reflected in the gentle waves of his model's hair; the absence of colour in the snowdrops is both mirrored and overwhelmed by the pale glory of Jane Burden's exquisite flesh tones.

The Sussex Chair, 1865 (Victoria & Albert Museum, London). One of Morris & Co.'s most popular chairs, it managed to combine a traditional, solid feel with delicate frame work. In the background is Seddon's oak cabinet.

especially the distressed, broody passionate mythological portraits of the late 1880s like *Prosperine* and the subject of Morris's anguish expressed covertly through the imagery of his prose and poetry.

Jane Burden described Morris as '... short, burly, corpulent, very careless and unfinished in his dress ... a delicate sensitive genius'. He was slightly unkempt and gauche but, after the charming Rossetti's departure for the winter Morris seemed to win her over by his dedicated sense of romance. They married in April 1859, Morris aged twenty-five, and Jane aged eighteen. For Morris this marriage was a further declaration of rebellion against accepted Victorian values, marrying for love and out of his class; the wedding was a romantic notion made real, as though Arthur and Guinevere had stepped out of their medieval tales while Lancelot was away on some heroic mission. The poet Swinburne declared, 'having that wonderful and most perfect stunner of his – to look at or speak to. The idea of his marrying her is insane. To kiss her feet is the utmost men should dream of doing.' After a six-week honeymoon they started a five-year period of contentment in the Red House, Bexley Heath. Rossetti meanwhile married his lover of ten years, Lizzie Siddal, who in her time had been an early and vivacious Pre-Raphaelite inspiration.

The Firm and The Red House

The year 1861 saw the founding of Morris, Marshall, Faulkner & Co., Fine Art Workmen in Painting, Carving, Furniture and the Metals, referred to by contemporaries as The Firm. With Morris as the main source of funds, the company included Rossetti, Burne-Jones, Arthur Hughes, Ford Madox Brown, P.P. Marshall, Faulkner and Philip Webb. They started in Red Lion Square, moving to Queen Square in 1865. One of their first pieces was a cabinet now housed at the Victoria & Albert Museum. It was a solid piece of workmanship designed by Webb and painted by Morris featuring a deep crimson, dragon's blood, interior.

One of the hallmarks of The Firm was the collaborative sense of vision which found its origins in the design and building of the home for the Morrises, the Red House, their 'palace of art'. Designed by Webb its Gothic porches, steep tiled roof and open construction represented a dramatic break from Victorian tradition. The Red House became the embodiment of Morris's philosophy of life and led naturally to The Firm. Burne-Jones said later that they decided to found '... a manufactory of all things necessary for decoration of a house. Webb had already designed some beautiful table glass ... metal candlesticks, and tables for the Red House, and I had already designed several windows for churches, so the idea grew of putting our experiences together for the service of the public.'

It was here that the first tangible expressions of comprehensive, living design were expressed, with glasswork, metalwork, carpentry, painting, wallpapers, tapestries, carpets and wall hangings, and tiles all harnessed into the service of the total interior design. Excessive ornamentation of decor was removed with only useful things being made and displayed; Burne-Jones's wife commented, 'The walls were bare, and the floors, nor could Morris have endured any chair, table, sofa or bed, not any hangings as were then in existence ... For the walls of other rooms than the drawing room (with its frescos by Burne-Jones) Morris designed flower patterns which his wife worked in wool on a dark ground, everything had to be useful and good to look at.' In one of his later lectures Morris said, 'to my mind it is only here and there out of the kitchen that you can find in a well-to-do house things that are of any use at all'. The gardens reflected the influence of his visits to Northern France and Belgium with roses growing across wattled fences, revelling in the deep sunshine.

Torment and Escape

For five years at The Red House the Morrises lived in a state of bliss. Their friends came to see them at weekends, they laughed, they had their two children, Jenny being born in 1861, and their second, May, coming a year later. But the canker of unrequited love returned to eat at their lives. Lizzie Siddal died from an overdose of laudanum and slowly the Lancelot Rossetti returned to claim the heart of his Guinevere Jane. There have been a number of biographical interpretations which suggest that Jane Burden married Morris in order to retain the elevation of society she had achieved by sitting for the glittering group of painters after Rossetti's departure from Oxford in 1858. Indeed Morris's only surviving painting of Burden is an unwittingly prophetic work. He painted her as Ysolde, or Iseult, the unfaithful bride of Mark, King of Cornwall. The central figure is often criticized for its awkwardness, but her wooden gait serves as a dramatic counterpoint to the lushly detailed, carefully decorated background. She is a woman out of sympathy with her landscape, preparing herself for marriage to one man, Mark, while yearning for another, Tristram.

The intense entanglement of affection and betrayal between Morris and Rossetti is difficult to portray over any distance in time but the clues to the desperate emotional tensions appear in the writings of them both.

In 1871 they jointly leased Kelmscott Manor, set in the clover meadows of Oxford, surrounded by orchards and fields and a river which ran into the Thames. Burden sat again for Rossetti and it is from

Pelican design for stained glass, by Burne-Jones, *c.* 1880. This Burne-Jones design is typical of the preparations for Morris & Co.'s stained glass. It's lush, fluid lines are characteristic of both the style of Burne-Jones himself and The Firm's preoccupation with natural subjects.

Design for carpet, undated (Victoria & Albert Museum, London). Customers at the Oxford Street showroom would be shown finished samples and paintings of carpet designs like this. The design shows the bold lines and curves, which were necessary for carpet patterns to achieve their effect, the small intricate patterns of a tapestry would have been lost when placed on a floor.

this time that the abundant, moody portraits which include *Prosperine* (the mortal imprisoned with the King of the Underworld, a reference of course to Morris) were painted. Their previous romantic affair flourished here and Morris found himself living an impossible double life with both his wife and hero-friend-partner, echoing the classic love triangles of Lancelot, Arthur and Guenevere, Tristram, Ysolde and Mark. During this period Morris published the escapist romances of *The Earthly Paradise* and *The Life and Death of Jason* and reviewed, favourably, Rossetti's *Willowwood* Sonnets of 1868.

It was an escape from the complexity, failure and emotional torture of his marriage that took Morris, with Charles Faulkner, on his first trip to Iceland. This became the next major influence on his life. The nature of the people, their culture and their landscape were radically different from his own emotional struggles and the extravagant, diseased English society he left behind. Grim Icelandic stoicism in the face of natural hardship provided a refreshing inspiration for both his poetry and his increasingly acute criticisms of the Victorian age. 'I learned a lesson there ... that the most grinding poverty is a trifling evil compared to the inequality of the classes.' His rugged translations of Icelandic sagas started at this time, including early works such as *Volsunga Saga,* which were highly regarded and well reviewed.

As the 1860s gave way to the following decade Rossetti and Jane's affair moved inexorably from obsessive attraction to depression, leading to several suicide attempts by Rossetti in the early 1870s and later, the complete collapse of Jane's health. In 1874 Rossetti was forced to leave Kelmscott as madness and depression became inseparable, moving to Cornwall with Jane for a time and painting perhaps the most evocative portrait of his obsession, *Asarte Syriaca.*

In direct contrast to Morris's personal life, The Firm was becoming a major commercial success. The drain on Morris's own financial resources however forced him to reconstitute Morris & Co. under his primary ownership. Rossetti and others were removed after a long and bitter struggle, and Rossetti died in 1882, broken and ashamed by his unrequited love.

Escape and Poetry

Much of Morris's early poetry was escapist. The inner turbulence, caused by his wife's love for Rossetti and the complications that arose from the friendships, business partnership and the personal insecurities that well within all artists, created an impressive canon of poetic work through which Morris sublimated his feelings. It is tempting to suggest that Morris's designs too, with their Hopkinsesque spring

The Sussex Chair, *c.* **1865**
(Victoria & Albert Museum, London).
The single-seat Sussex design spawned
a number of related pieces, including
this three-seat settee.

tensed patterns, taut with energy and colour, reflect the turmoil of his mind. It is most transparently evident though through his tapestry-like poetry, riven with loss, and it is here that we can see how he really felt. The recounting of classical tales and Icelandic myths dwells on sadness and suppressed love, in his melancholically titled *Love is Enough* he entreated the reader to allow him,

> *to build a shadowy isle of bliss*
> *Midmost the beating of the steely sea.*
> Love is Enough, *1872*

To modern ears and eyes much of his poetry is leaden (it is difficult to wrestle with the archaisms and heavy rhythms) but during his lifetime he was a celebrated poet, widely read and appreciated. He was offered the Chair of Poetry at Oxford in 1877 and later in life turned down the post of Poet Laureate on the death of Tennyson. His method is characterized by his dismissiveness for he never really valued the skill, sensing that for him it was 'a mere matter of craftsmanship'. He

Design for patchwork embroidery, undated (Victoria & Albert Museum, London). Such drawings were carried out to perfect the composition of the final work.

was not moved by inspiration like Keats before him or contemporaries like Thomas Hardy and his style drew on a quasi-medieval language which has a certain charm but is highly derivative.

His earliest poetry had been light romances, full of knights and ladies, lively and uncomplicated. With *The Earthly Paradise*, a series of related poems on an obviously escapist theme, he achieved great acclaim on publication between 1868 and 1870 and as with much of his poetry it drags an undertow of bitter, transient love. *The Earthly Paradise*, the Month Poems of which are considered to be his best verse, was written in the yearning, painful grind of emotional turmoil.

> *There, the lights gleam, and all is dark without !*
> *And in the sudden change our eyes meet dazed*
> *O look, love, look again ! the veil of doubt*
> *Just for one flash, past counting, then was raised !*
> *O eyes of heaven, as clear they sweet should blazed*
> *On mine a moment ! O come back again*
> *Strange rest and dear amid the long dull pain !*
> *January*, The Earthly Paradise, *1868–70*

With the emphatic pleas, the pitiful yearning, these tense, powerful lines speak of a relationship that has collapsed and cannot be rescued. Overall the epic sequence is a conscious foil to Chaucer's *The Canterbury Tales* whose medieval style Morris adopts but whose lip-smacking delight in life he studiously avoids. Morris's travellers do not reach their intended destination but the reader is invited to understand the transcendent power of art in delivering the earthly paradise which the harsh realities of life cannot. During this period he started an unfinished novel about two brothers who fell in love with the same woman – a subject of course which in life was all too real. *The Earthly Paradise* had been preceded by a long poem originally intended for inclusion within it, *The Life and Death of Jason*, which is a reinterpretation of the classic myth, tangible and delightful in its imagery. Indeed that most sonorous of poets Swinburne wrote in 1875, 'The pictures are clear and chaste, sweet and lucid, as early Italian work. There are crowds and processions, battle-pieces, and merry-makings, worthy of Benozzo and Carpaccio, single figures or groups of lovers, in a flowery waterland, worthy of Sandro or Filippino ... Rarely but in ballad and romance has such poetry been written, so broad and sad and simple.'

> *There comes a murmur from the shore,*
> *And in the close two fair streams are,*
> *Drawn from the purple hills afar,*
> *Drawn down unto the restless sea:*
> *Dark hills whose heath-bloom feeds no bee,*
> *Dark shore no ship has ever seen,*
> *Tormented by the billows green*
> *Whose murmur comes unceasingly*
> *Unto the place for which I cry'*
> *'A Garden by the Sea'*,
> The Life and Death of Jason, *1867*

Design for Honeysuckle fabric, 1874
(Birmingham City Museum). This
intense, sumptuous watercolour, ink
and pencil sketch comes from Morris's
most productive and innovative period
as a designer. It is one of his most
popular fabric designs and shows the
exquisite detail of his method through
the solid colour of the pattern's core.

The 1871 Icelandic trip heralded a major change in his life coinciding with the end of the artistic influence of Rossetti. Morris turned mournfully to the rigorous, natural honesty of the old Icelandic sagas which he translated throughout the rest of his life. One of the first was *The Hill of Venus*, his version of the Tannhäuser legend where a man awakens from a dream of love and is struck with the cold winds of reality. His poetic language reflected the change in subject and influence, moving away from the ornamented romanticism and classical mythology of his earlier work. The dreamy escape of *The Earthly Paradise* moved to the ugliness of real life and eventually to the concerted struggle for social change in later writings of *News from Nowhere*.

Four years later, 1875 saw the publication of his translations of the *Aeneid*, followed by the well received *Sigurd the Volsung*, but from this point on, he concentrated on the success of Morris & Co. As Henry James said, poetry was a 'sub-trade' for Morris, his real work being in The Firm. Jane became a shadow in his life, retreating sullenly into herself for the rest of her days. Henry James met her in the early 1880s and referred to her as 'an apparition of fearful and wonderful intensity ... a thin, pale face, a pair of sad, deep dark, Swinburnian eyes ...' But Morris seemed unwilling to be destroyed by the lovelessness, or the industrial madness of the society around him. He raged and explored with endless determination to overcome personal and societal affliction, producing poetry, designs and instruction of immense warmth and timelessness. During this time, his most productive artistic period, he became the greatest of all English pattern designers.

CHAPTER 2

Artist, Craftsman, Designer

In the early 1870s, Morris harnessed the personal crises of his private life and mounted a renewed assault on the artistic and social ramparts of accepted Victorian thought. He established a pre-eminence as a pattern designer and began an exceptional and influential series of designs.

Overleaf:
Wey, 1884 (William Morris Gallery, London). The Wey Chintz, named after the River Wey in Surrey, England, is a highly satisfying repeating pattern and reflected Morris's fascination with English rivers.

The mechanism of Morris's creativity was the success of The Firm. The reconstitution of the company under his sole ownership in 1873 freed him to act as he knew he should. Of the original partners, Rossetti, Ford Madox Brown and Faulkner had not contributed much in the previous years and were eventually, and resentfully, paid off with one thousand pounds compensation. William Morris and his manager George Wardle continued to run the company with Morris, Philip Webb and Burne-Jones designing most of the objects. Indeed Burne-Jones was happy to keep designing and certainly had no thoughts of managing or organizing; he said later that he would rather live in a picture than in life. His work was wan and romantic, less sturdy than Morris's own designs and more rooted in a literary sense of medieval inspiration.

Morris's rare combination of intellectual, artistic and practical skills enabled The Firm to become an impressive and expanding business, aiming to gain commissions for complete interior decoration. In April 1876 he opened a showroom in a suitably modish part of London, on the corner of Oxford Street and North Audley Street, where customers were shown samples, pattern books, photographs and sketches for wallpapers, tapestries, embroideries, carpets and complete interior designs. The Firm produced glass goblets, wrought-iron bedsteads, stained-glass windows, solid, burnished tables and functional chairs such as those still referred to as the 'Morris chair'. They decorated private homes, public places, even royal palaces. For several years they also undertook commissions for stained-glass windows, including the stunning design, *The Last Judgement,* for the West window in St Philip's Cathedral, Birmingham. It was in such religious subjects that the powerful, compelling energies of Morris and his Firm united so successfully with a commitment to organic decoration in places of worship. Their windows did not attempt to replicate the past, merely to capture its spirit. Many different artists and craftsmen worked on them, with Burne-Jones normally designing the figures, Webb and Morris decorating the foregrounds. But it was always Morris who determined the colours and the lead lines and he provided a crafted integrity which held true to the materials. The collaborative designs of Morris and Burne-Jones in this field between 1869 and 1875 are regarded as some of the greatest works of the late Victorian Gothic revival.

Other commissions undertaken by The Firm included the radiant working of wool, silk and gold thread in the *Romance and the Rose* tapestry designs, with figures by Burne-Jones and decorative backgrounds by Morris. The two also combined to create *Poesia, Musica* and *The Musicians,* for the Royal School of Needlework, newly opened in 1872, where their fresh, open designs became instrumental in liberating embroidery from mechanical canvaswork patterns.

Philosophy and Inspiration in Design

Morris's contribution to the long historical line of great art is very difficult to isolate. During a highly productive life he wrestled with many different forms of art, from murals to oil paintings, calligraphy to stained glass design, embroidery to carpets, illuminated manuscripts to furniture design. The potency of his cultural impact lies in the whole man and the whole man embraced a whole concept of life which expressed itself though the many different media. Morris's art, writing and politics form an entire body of work which needs to be considered as a whole vision but it is possible to consider him through the most accessible of his creative impulses, his pattern designs.

Within the bold, two-dimensional patterns Morris released and crafted a visceral response to the curves and waves of nature; they surge through the motifs of *Willow* (1874) and the rhythms of *Honeysuckle* (1876). They formulate his rejection of the inert, vulgar art of the age, like the oil paintings of Sir Frederick Leighton and the mechanically, mass-produced decorative objects. Morris later articulated this response,

Indian Diaper, 1875. This was one of the first Morris wallpapers to use the indigo discharge method. Morris's papers were highly regarded because of their organic patterns, which seemed to keep growing on the walls.

Bird and Vine, 1879. From the late 1870s Morris's wallpapers were less satisfying, suffering perhaps from his concentration on other textiles and the dual use of designs for both wallpapers and fabrics. *Bird and Vine*, however, was a stately pattern and well received at the time.

encapsulating his philosophies of design, in the series of lectures starting with 'On the Lesser Arts' in 1877, stating defiantly that 'Nature is the basis of good art, good art is the basis of a moral society':

> *There is a great deal of sham work in the world, hurtful to the buyer, more hurtful to the seller, if only he knew it; most hurtful to the maker.*

Pleasure in the making, like the worship inherent in the carving of a gargoyle which would not be seen on a cathedral, came from toiling at the worthwhile, understanding the materials, observing nature and shaping it to be true to itself, not by forcing ornamentation for the sake of it. This Ruskinian belief in an art which meant something was taken a step further in Morris as he dedicated himself to mastering the techniques of all the crafts he pursued. He took this principle still further by perceiving it as a need and a method for forcing a change in society.

He declared that 'real art is the expression by man of his pleasure in labour' and a study of Morris's work and his writings on decorative art surrenders an intense, almost physical relish in the sinews and rolls of the natural landscape. He seemed to design from within rather than separate from the natural world, readily embracing the organic imperfections and chaotic exuberances of vines and leaves, then fashioning them in the two-dimensional forms of wallpapers, panels and textiles. In *Trellis* (1862) he faithfully reinterpreted the trellises of his rose garden at The Red House and *Daisy*, his first wallpaper created shortly after, shows an early desire to harness the formalism of man's instincts and apply it to the novelty and freedom of living forms.

If we really care about art we shall not put up with something or other, but shall choose honest whitewash instead, on which sun and shadow play so pleasantly.

Morris warned against bad design, especially when it deviated from natural inspirations. He also maintained that a good artist must 'Follow nature, study antiquity, make (his) own art', because, as part of the natural world man's own informed response to it and development from it was as natural as the form and beauty of the flowers and the fields. His use of the past elaborated, then turned into a pattern of his own can be seen in the series of wallpapers and chintzes based on rivers, such *Evenlode* (1883) and *Wandle* (1884). Rivers, particularly the

Acanthus and Vine, 1879
(A.F. Kerstung). Morris's first tapestry was woven by him at Kelmscott where he deliberately looked back to the work of medieval Flemish weavers.

Sunflower, 1879 (Victoria & Albert Museum, London). A flowing, majestic wallpaper pattern with the typical interplay of large motifs and more subtle flowing tendrils.

Opposite:
Minstrel, Burne-Jones, 1882-4 (Victoria & Albert Museum, London). This unusual stained-glass window features, characteristically, a central figure designed by the highly experienced Edward Burne-Jones.

Thames, were a major source of inspiration to him gliding through many of his works, providing energy, refreshment, transport and a touch of other-worldly magic. The Thames washed past his Hammersmith home, which he moved to in 1878, and up towards Kelmscott and the Oxford countryside he loved so dearly.

For all his restless striving Morris was often a studious and disciplined man. At the South Kensington (later renamed the Victoria & Albert) Museum he researched sources ranging from the manuscripts of a French contemporary of Chaucer, Froissart, to Italian and Elizabethan renaissance textile patterns. In 1882 he gave evidence to the Royal Commission on Technical Instruction:

> *However original a man may be, he cannot afford to disregard the works of art that have been produced in times past when design was flourishing; he is bound to study old examples, but he is also bound to supplement that by a careful study of nature, because if he does not he will certainly fall into a sort of cut and dried conventional method of designing.*

This study of the past yielded a richness and depth to Morris's patterns, a sensuousness which was entirely missing from many of his contemporaries' designs. The buds of the *Honeysuckle*, the leaves of the *Acanthus*, the birds of *Strawberry Thief* seemed to whisper of their origins, creating a *trompe l'oeil* of all the senses. Morris's skill was to combine inspiration with true craftsmanship. He harnessed the raw materials he worked into the service of the subject he was creating. The woven stitches of the *Holy Grail* tapestry create the textured background of bark, leaves and grasses. He insisted of artists that they should 'try to get the most out of your material, but always in a way which honours it most. Not only should it be obvious what your material is but something should be done with it which is specially natural to it, something that could not be done with any other.' This was in part a reaction to the overpolished, ornate furniture of the period which disguised the wood it was created from to such an extent that it could have been anything. The brute force of manufacture in being able to make smooth rounded surfaces from almost any object was, to Morris, a travesty of beauty, ignorant of the serendipity in the shaping of oak or beech or walnut.

Although his methods prefigured twentieth-century experimentation with expressionistic shapes and colours, Morris had no affinity with purely abstract patterns, demanding 'plenty of meaning in your patterns; I must have unmistakable suggestions of gardens and fields, strange trees and boughs and tendrils.' It was a fine balance though because he also rejected simple replication, seeking a sense of hidden depth, a sense of light just beyond the next corner in his own and

Design for **Evenlode, 1883.** The river Evenlode runs through Morris's beloved Oxfordshire countryside, flowing into the Thames. It inspired this wallpaper design and it is possible to see the intricate rippling and dance of the water in the tumbling, repeating patterns.

others' designs, 'In all patterns that are meant to fill the eye and satisfy the mind, there should be a sense of mystery. We should not be able to reach the whole thing at once, nor desire to do so, nor be compelled by that desire to go on tracing line after line to find out how a pattern is made.' The natural world is bound in this way, with each tree and flower part of a seamless interconnecting stream of colour and texture from which the eye scalpels a small section. Bad design is immediately self-contained, enslaved by its two-dimensional form. Morris's success lies in transcending the limitations of the form and finding methods to echo the spirit of his subject. Patterns by definition repeat themselves but, as in *Pimpernel* of 1875, hiding the geometry enables the eye to follow one line of colour, be interrupted by a burgeoning leaf which leads away to still another line. Morris worked hard at perfecting the vigorous clarity of his patterns. 'It is with a pattern as with a fortress, it is no stronger than its weakest point,' for the eye would always light on the weakness. This would apply as much to a wallpaper, intended to envelope a room as to an embroidered cushion with its more restricted definition. For both extremes the pattern had to flow. The allure of

Morris's techniques also derives from the adaptation of his own designs through the different media; many of the wallpaper designs became chintzes and tapestries, forming a cohesive potential scheme for his interior decorations with the subtle, weaving exchange of motif and colour between his wallpaper, fabrics and textiles.

Textiles and Interiors

Morris's continuing appeal rests on the rich variety of designs he produced for a range of textile goods. He executed over thirty original designs many of which are among the finest of their kind and are regarded by some as significant works in the history of art. Unlike wallpapers, textiles are based more on colour and pattern because as upholstery or wallhangings they are rarely seen flat. To gain the most from the thread and the colours Morris returned to the techniques of the past. This was not simply a reaction to the industrial methods of the day but also a response to the quality of what was produced. A demand for high standards lay behind many of his actions, particularly when it came to making textiles.

Mechanization had brought major changes in the production of textiles from the late 1700s so that by the Great Exhibition a huge range of goods was shown as both affordable and brightly coloured. Up to the mid-1700s wooden blocks were used to print patterns on cotton but

Honeysuckle II, 1876 (Victoria & Albert Museum, London). The honeysuckle provided the inspiration for a number of Morris's designs for fabrics and wallpapers; this one is a repeating pattern from his greatest period of wallpaper design.

these were superseded by copper plates which carried more detail. Both techniques though were hugely time-consuming with a printer only able to make six pieces of twenty-eight yard cloths in a week. The advent of steam brought a terrific increase of speed as the copper plates were wrapped around rollers and rolled across the yards of cloth. With advances in cheaper, quicker drying inks, the whole process moved to the production of five hundred pieces a day at a time when the expanding British Empire was giving manufacturers access to previously unheard of countries, expanding the demand and fuelling new advances in inks and printing.

Volume did not equal quality. The priority of the manufacturers in the swelling market was to make profit by filling a need rather than taking care with the craft. The dynamic of their businesses did not allow them to think too hard in the way that Morris demanded. His designs required depth of colour and variety which only the older dyes and blocking methods seemed to be able to deliver. He wanted to return to natural vegetable dyes like indigo blue and the insect dyes like red kermes, perfectly consistent with his attempt to unify method with subject, complementing the beauty and rigour of the natural world. He learnt about old dyeing techniques and with his customary vigour he set about mastering them in order to design effectively for the textiles for which they would be used. He claimed that 'Anyone wanting to produce dyed textiles with any artistic quality in them must entirely forego the modern and commercial methods in favour of those which are as old as Pliny, who speaks of them as being old in his time.' Having discovered the printer Thomas Wardle in Leek, Staffordshire, he spent several weeks experimenting. Slowly they perfected the techniques, with trial strips of cloth being sent between them, Morris exposing the results to sunlight or matching them against older materials. Eventually, by mixing natural dyes with some modern chemical inks, they achieved success. *Honeysuckle* (1876), *Marigold* (1875) and *Larkspur* (1872) all date from this time and show an integrity of purpose quite alien to contemporary design. It is worth noting that Morris was driven by the desire to achieve authenticity and although he generally assumed that the older methods were best he would readily adopt new methods and materials as required.

Morris also experimented with other printing techniques, notably the indigo discharge method which lent the designs a subliminal unity. The cloth was dipped in the indigo dye first then pattern blocks with bleach were pressed on to it, followed by the application of the appropriate colours on further blocks. *Strawberry Thief* (1883) dates from this period and is perhaps his most enduring pattern. Experimentation also continued in the patterns, with *Acanthus* (1880) and *African Marigold* (1876) being among the first examples of a hypnotic mirrored design.

Wandle, 1884. This wallpaper was named, with affection, after the River Wandle, which ran through the Merton Abbey works and which was used to wash the cloth.

Overleaf:
Bullerswood, 1889 (Victoria & Albert Museum, London). This hand-knotted woollen carpet was probably a collaboration between Morris and D.H. Dearle, and it was also the last carpet on which Morris worked.

Wardle printed many of Morris's fabrics but remote supervision had always proved to be unsatisfactory, never a guarantee of consistently high standards. In 1877 Morris moved a loom into Queen Square and made *Peacock and Dragon* (1878), *Bird* (1880) and, later, *Anemone* here. In 1881 The Firm moved to the seven-acre site of Merton Abbey in Surrey where there was more space for the cloth and powered looms. Having achieved the effects he required Morris was perfectly happy using new methods of manufacture whereby he could make excellent goods and enable his craftsmen to benefit from their own work without compromising their ability to earn a living with others. He was not anti-machine as such but opposed to the use of machines to make profit alone.

The Firm was involved in the manufacture of a great number of other textiles, but Morris in his mature years was enthralled by the making of tapestries:

> *The noblest of the weaving arts is the Tapestry: in which there is nothing mechanical: it may be looked upon as a mosaic of pieces of colour made up of dyed threads, and is capable of producing wall ornament of any degree of elaboration within the proper limits of duly considered decorative work.*

It attracted him because it was a great 'medieval art'. *Cabbage and Vine* and *Woodpecker* of 1885 represent pure attempts by Morris to perfect this art, but later in his life all the tapestries were collaborative efforts with Burne-Jones primarily designing the figures, Morris, Webb and D.H. Dearle, the senior employed designer contributing background or decorative detail. *The Forest* (1887) is thought to have been worked on by all four and there is some debate about its real quality. Many of the best-known tapestries drew their inspiration directly from Mallory's *Mort d'Arthur*, including *Adoration* and the striking, lambency of *Holy Grail* which was a huge collaborative achievement from 1890–4. Designed for Stanmore Hall in Middlesex the commission was for six panels to hang from the cornice with verdures hanging beneath them to the skirting boards. Dreamy knights gaze wistfully at their maidens, the background cloth is gently and subtly medieval with ochres, creams and indigos providing very detailed examples of The Firm's method of tapestry craftsmanship. Morris only contributed the heraldic devices with Burne-Jones providing the main figure work.

In contrast to the detailed figure and decorative work of tapestries, The Firm's designs for carpets relied on blocks of colour and suggestions of shape. *Lily*, *Bellflower* and *Rose* of 1875–6 had established Morris as a pre-eminence on carpet design and he was appointed as Art Referee to the Victoria & Albert Museum to help with acquisitions. He aimed 'to make England independent of the East for

I once a king and chief · now am the tree-barks thief :

ever twixt trunk and leaf · chasing the prey ·

Woodpecker, 1885 (William Morris Gallery, London). The high warp tapestry of *Woodpecker* is a beautifully powerful working of imagination and nature. The interleaving of Morris's own verse, with vines, flowers, fruit and the woodpecker itself is characteristic of the style of Morris & Co. from around this period.

carpets that may lay claim to being works of art', intending to arrest the cheapening quality of manufactured work. The Firm's move to Merton Abbey facilitated the manufacture of large-scale carpets such as the 39-foot-long, 12-foot-wide *Clouds* (1887) and *Bullerswood* (1889), both of which showed Morris at his decorative best. *Bullerswood* was his last carpet for The Firm (which produced many fine examples under D.H. Dearle's subsequent stewardship) and he concentrated on tapestries.

As early as 1866 Morris's Firm had decorated the armoury and tapestry rooms at St James's Palace and a year later they also designed the Green Dining Room at the Victoria & Albert Museum. But it was the 1880s which saw Morris finally established as the supreme interior decorator of his age. His wallpapers and chintzes were highly fashionable, with wealthy clients like the Greek merchant Alexander Ionedes commissioning him to decorate his house in Holland Park. He decorated some of the first-class cabins on the Titanic, the Webb-designed house of Clouds in Wiltshire (for which the carpet of the same name had been commissioned) and the interior

Wightwick Manor, Wolverhampton. The outside view of the Manor shows the strongly Gothic influence on its construction, entirely sympathetic with Morris's own inclinations. The owner, Theodore Mander, was a paint manufacturer and a keen follower of Ruskin.

of Theodore Mander's Wightwick Manor in Staffordshire. This last scheme is particularly interesting because Mander had also been influenced by John Ruskin's cultural critiques and built his own house with the honesty and integrity of the construction in full view, undisguised by ornamentation.

One of the major contradictions of Morris's life was that for all his beliefs in the quality and care of materials and the people who made them, primarily he manufactured his own goods for people who had no special sympathy for his philosophies. Many purchased the fabrics because it was fashionable to do so rather than because the goods were good or useful. Morris recognized this all too well, turning on the owner of Rounton Range, Sir Isaac Bell, one day declaiming his frustration 'that I spend my life in ministering to the swinish luxury of the rich!'

Nonetheless, Morris's search for beauty and honesty in art, design and poetry developed into a full-scale manifesto for change in his lectures and political writings.

Wightwick Manor, Wolverhampton.
The room is decorated with wallpaper, carpet and tiles based on *Honeysuckle* designs. Note the presence of a Morris & Co. Sussex Chair.

CHAPTER 3

Art and Society

The latter part of Morris's life was dominated by his passionate commitment to the need for change in society. From his early years he had always rebelled against the conventions of Victorian Society, the apathetic, unquestioning acceptance of industrial strength, but this developed into a vision of man and the environment which led him to act beyond mere intellectual criticism.

The year 1877 was important for Morris, marking the end of his most fertile period of wallpaper design. He gave his first lecture on art and society, refused a nomination as Professor of Poetry at Oxford University, wrote a rallying manifesto *'To the Working-men of England'* and started the Society for the Protection of Ancient Buildings. Each event is consistent with the thrust of his life, moving ineluctably towards a greater commitment to change in society. He developed into a highly perceptive social thinker, moving the arguments of Ruskin forward through the challenges of the late nineteenth century and into the twentieth.

The foundation of the Society for the Protection of Ancient Buildings grew from Morris's early convictions that the Victorian zeal for restoration was an unhealthy desire for uniformity, a return to an imagined original without understanding the organic nature of an old building. To Morris, the evolution of a building with, say, the replacement of buttress timbers in the seventeenth century was simply a natural process which should not be tampered with. He revered Salisbury Cathedral for its Gothic simplicity, worshipping 'the expression of reverence for nature, the life of man upon the earth'. The first meeting of the Society, which became known as the Anti-Scrape, was attended by, among others, Thomas Carlyle, Burne-Jones and Philip Webb. Anti-Scrape was responsible for saving a number of fine ancient buildings, including Peterborough Cathedral, the school buildings at Eton, and Westminster Abbey. A significant triumph of the Society's effect on Government thinking at the time was the passing of the Ancient Monument Protection Act of 1882 which drew important buildings into public ownership. Morris & Co.'s stained-glass projects for churches and cathedrals across England sustained the philosophy of the Society and the reasons for its existence, extending its intellectual analysis into the physical continuation of organic development, replacing old glass with no attempt at sentimental affection.

Commitment and Socialism

Morris's lectures on art, held initially in Kelmscott Manor and later published individually and in collected form, carry particular significance because in writing them Morris was forced to think through his instincts and articulate a credible vision of the interplay between art and society. The lectures represent one of the most impressive bodies of work in the history of English and European cultural development; he exposed the method behind his designs and he challenged the traditional approaches to decorative art, the way people lived with and used their art: he brought this together with the thinking of Ruskin to reveal the significance of art as a social force. To Morris art was not

Willow Bough, 1887 (Victoria & Albert Museum, London). A subtly naturalistic pattern which resonates with the movement and freshness of the natural world.

simply for pleasure but a moral force in itself, not just reflective of a society in the Ruskin analysis but a way of changing society, too. In trying to locate the position of art in society through these lectures, he became part of a movement that swept through Europe. The rise in industrial fortunes brought with them a nascent resentment and suffering of those on whose backs the growth was being made; the Victorian age was a capitalistic bludgeon, creating iniquities as quickly as it created wealth.

Morris's instincts, certainly Liberal and radical in his younger years, strove against this in his work and in his lectures. He brought together various strands of thinking but his analysis was not a simple return to ancient, medieval codes where craftsmanship was appreciated. He understood the value of work because he had buried himself in it in his attempts, for instance, to master the physical, messy technique of dyeing. He knew the reward and the struggle involved in good hard labour where the finished article said much about the craftsman's sense of self worth, as well as his benefit to the society for which he worked: 'The beauty of the handicrafts of the Middle Ages came from this, that the workman had control over his material, tools and time.' In such circumstances the art, the crafts produced became

Membership card for Democratic Federation, 1883 (Marx Memorial Library, London). Morris devoted his energies, money and design skills to the fulfilment of his dreams. The strikingly ornate membership card seems inappropriate for a struggling, campaigning organization but in fact the craftsmanship implied in the decoration is central to Morris's belief in the just pride of the working man.

truly valuable to all involved in the process. For Morris the inevitable consequence of the industrialization of manufacture was evident for all to see.

> *What tons of unutterable rubbish pretending to be works of art in some degree would this maxim clear out of our London house, if it were understood and acted upon! ... as a rule all the decoration (so called) that has got there is there for the sake of show, not because anybody likes it.*

The significance of this lies in his belief that art is necessary to man's essential happiness, that it is 'necessary to the life of man, if the progress of civilization is not to be as causeless as the turning of a wheel that makes nothing'. From this belief much flows and it becomes clear that art in its pure form, as both Ruskin and Morris saw it, must be a product of man being part of the process, not a dispensable form of tool. 'We should be masters of our machines and not their slaves, as now,' he declared. 'It is not this or that tangible steel and brass machine which we want to get rid of, but the great intangible machine of commercial tyranny, which oppresses the lives of us all.'

In his lifetime Morris was occasionally regarded as a crank who disliked machinery, who yearned for the simple life of the medieval craftsman. This was a convenient solution for the people who bought his fabrics and decorated their living rooms with his sumptuous cloths. The uncomfortable fact was that his dislike of machinery was a more sophisticated challenge to their own way of life than they wanted to admit. Increasingly the 'idle singer of an empty day', the writer of the escapist fantastist of *The Earthly Paradise* was ready to engage the grim realities of the lives of his fellow men rather than simply escape from them. The dreaming of his early work was radically overtaken in the late 1870s and early 1880s by a commitment to social change and the use of art as a moral instrument in that change. By 1882 he had travelled the short philosophical road from John Ruskin to Karl Marx.

In 'How I Became a Socialist', a major retrospective article in the Social Democratic Federation's *Justice*, in 1894, Morris wrote that 'Both historical studies and my practical conflict with the philistinism of modern society have forced on me the conviction that art cannot have a real life and growth under the present system of commercialism and profit-mongering. I have tried to develop this view, which is in fact Socialism seen through the eyes of an artist, in various lectures which I delivered in 1878.'

The commercialism and profit-mongering revealed a target for Morris's ascerbic and active tongue during the Balkan crisis of 1876 where the Tory Prime Minister Disraeli was leading the country into an alliance with Turkey, in order to protect the trade routes through to India. India was of course a huge new Imperial market for England and a provider of new materials. For the Government the issue was one of protecting the nation's interests. For Morris, and the Liberal opposition at the time, it had more to do with the nature of those with

Wallflower, *c.* **1890** (Victoria & Albert Museum, London). One of the later period wallpapers with *Bachelor's Button* and *Pink and Rose*.

whom Disraeli was proposing an alliance. Morris libellously called the Turks, 'a gang of thieves and murderers' and national co-operation for purely commercial reasons was unconscionable to him.

The year 1877 saw the publication of his first rallying call to labour – *To the Working-men of England*. The pamphlet savagely criticized the 'Tory rump' and the jingoistic newspapers who would drag the working man into an immoral war, using them in the same way that the profiteering factory owners used the working man as fodder. Though still a Liberal, by then he was already drifting from the compromise and double dealing inherent in the system of Government. At this time George Howell and Henry Broadhurst of the new Labour Representation League spoke out with similar views and Morris increasingly identified with their determined sense of rough justice. From this point on Morris's life collides with the early history of the Labour movement in England and he played an important part in the debate which led to dramatic change in parliamentary representation for working people.

Morris's strident, anti-capitalist views reviled the divisive nature of the Industrial Revolution which had overturned the natural order between those who possessed wealth, mainly through the ownership of land, and those who did not. His instinctive response as a designer and craftsman enabled him to understand the needs of people who worked with their hands for a living. He made no value judgements against one man's ability to produce above another and it was important that the fact of making was given a sense of worth in itself. The speeding up of processes, the technological advances which allowed machines to make goods more quickly and more perfectly, automatically distanced man from the work for which he was previously necessary. As machines became the producers of profit, the rapid accumulation of capital became an achievable goal for those with organizational ability, ideas and some money. The balance of power in society shifted dramatically, creating a new class of people who came to power from between the ancient divide of landowners and common people, by the express force of their commercial acumen and industrial success. Those men or women whose primary skill was to labour were reduced to simple button-pressers and lever-pullers. Craft and pride therein were disappearing, disenfranchising a huge section of society:

> ... the extensive use of machinery ... the work of the proletarians has lost all individual character and, consequently, all charm for the workman. He becomes an appendage of the machine.

Morris had hoped that the Liberals would address themselves to this but the 1880s brought Gladstone back into power without delivering the radical edge to reform which had been promised. A new solution was required and the Labour Representation League was

When Adam Delved and Eve Span, sketch for the frontispiece of *A Dream of John Bull* (Kelmscott Press, 1892). Burne-Jones's supreme ability for fluid figurework provided Morris with the perfect partner for his sometimes leaden writing. The two friends collaborated on many projects which allowed their respective skills to complement their strengths.

When Adam delved and Eve span
Who was then the gentleman

Vine, 1890 (Private Collection). Morris designed this embroidered hanging which was then sewn by May Morris and her assistants.

very much part of a continental shift in European thought born out of frustration and poverty.

In 1883, Morris read *Das Kapital*, in a French translation. He also lectured in Manchester, on *Wealth and Riches*, and in Oxford on *Art and Democracy*. Many in his position had criticized without acting and would have been happy lecturing and thinking anxiously, but Morris's gathering commitment led him to join the new Social Democratic Foundation (SDF). He funded many of their activities and he founded their newspaper, *Justice*, writing for it and selling it on the streets of Hammersmith. His studies of Marx brought a more severe focus to his commitment and *Das Kapital* influenced him profoundly, but he fashioned Marx's beliefs to suit his own views on the consummate power of art. Marx defined the reasons for Morris's distaste and defiance of Victorian values. He had much to say about the rights of the working man, but also the ineffable value in what is produced by him. He observed that industrial societies took what a man made and alienated it from him, forcing the unskilled to become yet poorer. Trade unions had started to help the labourers who had a unique skill to offer but in a society where labour was plentiful, the unskilled were not valued and so were easily oppressed. Marx in essence was a sympathetic man and cared deeply for the equality he espoused. Morris responded to this and became one of those who Marx identified as vital to the struggle, one of those 'bourgeoisie who goes over to the proletariat, a bourgeois ideologist who has raised themselves to the level of comprehending theoretically the historical movements of the whole'. 'I do not want art for a few, any more than education for a few or freedom for a few,' is one of Morris's most celebrated confirmations of his belief that those less educated than himself should nevertheless

The Saville Armchair, c. 1890 (William Morris Gallery, London). A later example of Morris and Co.'s furniture, combining the *Strawberry Thief* fabric with a sturdy wooden frame.

have the same opportunities that he did. In 1883 he wrote to his friend C.E. Maurice:

> *I do not believe in the world being saved by any system – I only assert the necessity of attacking systems grown corrupt, and no longer leading anywhither; that to my mind is the case with the present system of capital and labour: as all my lectures assert, I have personally been gradually driven to the conclusion that art has been handcuffed by it, and will die out of civilisation if the system lasts ...*

In 1884 he set up the Hammersmith branch of the SDF, and worked robustly for the cause of change. May Morris, his second daughter, began to take a much greater part in the running of The Firm in the mid-1880s, supervising and designing the embroidery section in particular. She was an ardent supporter both of her adored father and his causes, campaigning with him on street corners and engaging in the political debates. She became a critical supporting influence in his life because although Rossetti had died in 1882 the damage to the Morrises' marriage was irreparable. In 1884 Morris left the SDF and formed the Socialist League and started their magazine, *Commonweal*. He lectured 120 times in the two years that followed, covering the whole country, ready to speak on democracy, art and the people, translating, ironically, Homer, while travelling on the train.

During the late 1880s Morris took part in many of the incidents that led to the creation of Socialism as a true political force. Although he was labelled by Engels as a 'settled, sentimental socialist', he participated in many of the street disturbances and rallies of the time. He was arrested for incitement and obstruction and later took an active part in the terrible events of what became known as Bloody Sunday, 13 November 1887. This was the culmination of the confrontations that autumn when the full power of organized capital, the police and the army, tore into the weak and ragged ranks of labour. The naïve idealism of people like Morris was severely undermined causing some to turn to constitutional means of change, through Parliament and the growth of the evolutionary Socialism of the Fabian Society, while others became increasingly anarchic. Divisions in the Socialist movement forced Morris's departure from the Socialist League although he continued to help individuals, and published one of his greatest written works, the prose romance, *News from Nowhere*, through the medium of *Commonweal*. Bernard Shaw said at the time, 'Morris, who had been holding the League up by the scruff of the neck, opened his hand, whereupon it dropped like a stone into the sea, leaving only a little wreckage to come to the surface occasionally, a demand for bail at a police court or a small loan.'

Morris's bed at Kelmscott Manor, 1890. The hangings around Morris's bed were embroidered by May Morris and her team, which included W.B. Yeats's sister Lily. The text is, once again, verse by Morris himself.

Morris's writing had continued throughout this period, including the rather lumpen prose of the Socialist fantasy *A Dream of John Bull* and a masterpiece of disillusionment, *News From Nowhere*. Nowhere is the strict translation of the Greek, *Utopia*, but Morris describes the achievement of the perfect state only after a bitter civil war. In it he looks forward prophetically into the twentieth century, but ultimately the story takes us back to the hapless, fractured time of his writing where he enjoins the reader to 'Go on living while you may, striving, with whatsoever pain and labour needs must be, to build up little by little the new day of fellowship, and rest, and happiness.' This is a rather miserable legacy after the preceding delights of the countryside during the prose journey, the fresh, joyful relief in the new, imagined society, but is consistent with Morris's increasing weariness with the scale of his own impact and the inability of international Socialism to deliver a lasting solution.

In 1891 Morris, at the age of fifty-seven, suffered a stroke from which he never fully recovered. In spite of this he made several public appearances, speaking on the same platform as Shaw and Engels at the May Day rally of 1892. In that year the disparate strands of Socialism reunited briefly and their joint efforts contributed to the historic election of three independent Labour Party members to Parliament. Shortly after, Kier Hardie, the most celebrated of the creators of the British Labour movement, invited Morris to become leader of the Labour Party, an honour which he declined because of his faltering health.

One of Morris's most fascinating and lucid works is the article written for *Justice* in 1894, two years before his death. Entitled, *Why I Became a Socialist*, it is important because during the preceding years the Socialist movement had been afflicted with schisms as the vanguard of new challenge came to terms with the methods of the old world and, in assimilating itself to the parliamentary methods of election and persuasion it became a more cohesive, but less explosive force.

> *Was it all to end in a counting-house on top of the cinder heap ... a Whig committee dealing out champagne to the rich and margarine to the poor in such convenient portions as would make all men contented together, though the pleasure of the eyes was gone from the world ...*
>
> Why I Became a Socialist, *1894*

Morris's hatred of squalor and inequality, of bad art and low self-esteem, of exploitation and the tastelessness of the middle class of his age kept him passionate and angry about society. Socialism was a religion for him and the injustices which gave rise to his convictions

Opposite and above:
Bachelor's Button, 1892 (Victoria & Albert Museum, London). Many of Morris's designs were produced in different colours, using the same copper blocks rolled on to paper. This is perhaps his most successful pattern of the later years, made in both red and blue.

sustained him through the difficulties which ravaged the movement in its early years.

> ... *the study of history, and the love and the practice of art forced me into a hatred of the civilisation which, if things were to stop as they are, would turn history into inconsequent nonsense, and make art a collection of the curiosities of the past, which would have no serious relation to the life of the present.*
>
> Why I Became a Socialist

The Kelmscott Press

In contrast to the gritty, street corner vigour of his public life Morris developed a significant interest in book printing and typography in the late 1880s. His earlier fascination with illuminated manuscripts in the Bodleian Library had remained with him for much of his life; he amassed an impressive collection of beautiful bound books, including a *Twelfth Century English Book of Hours* which cost four hundred pounds – a small fortune at the time. The prospect of producing modern, printed versions of such books brought together many of his fascinations and represented tangible evidence of his sense of function in art because they could be designed by hand from the nature of the paper, the colour of the ink, the style of typography and the subject matter itself. The repeated patterns, the loving care required to make an object which was at once beautiful and useful, the joy which could be experienced both by the maker and the reader, these were central to Morris's method of creating. An indication of his high regard for such books is that he compared them to the supreme form of art and function in his lecture on Gothic architecture in 1889: 'The only work of art which surpasses a complete medieval book is a complete medieval building.'

After the publication of *The Earthly Paradise* in 1874 Morris had started a project to print and bind a decorated version, but with over a hundred designs completed by Burne-Jones he abandoned it for other pursuits. The late 1880s revived his interest and he oversaw the printing of his romances, *The House of the Wolfungs* (1888) and *The Roots of the Mountains* (1889). The Icelandic Sagas lent themselves to the contrast of heavy black type on spartan white paper and it was his experiments with subject and form which led him to extend his growing interest in typography and create, in 1891, the Kelmscott Press. It was not intended to be a commercial proposition but a celebration and revival of medieval arts. The first book produced, his own *Glittering Plain*, was planned as a very short run for friends but the demand was much higher than expected. Despite fears for quality on the higher

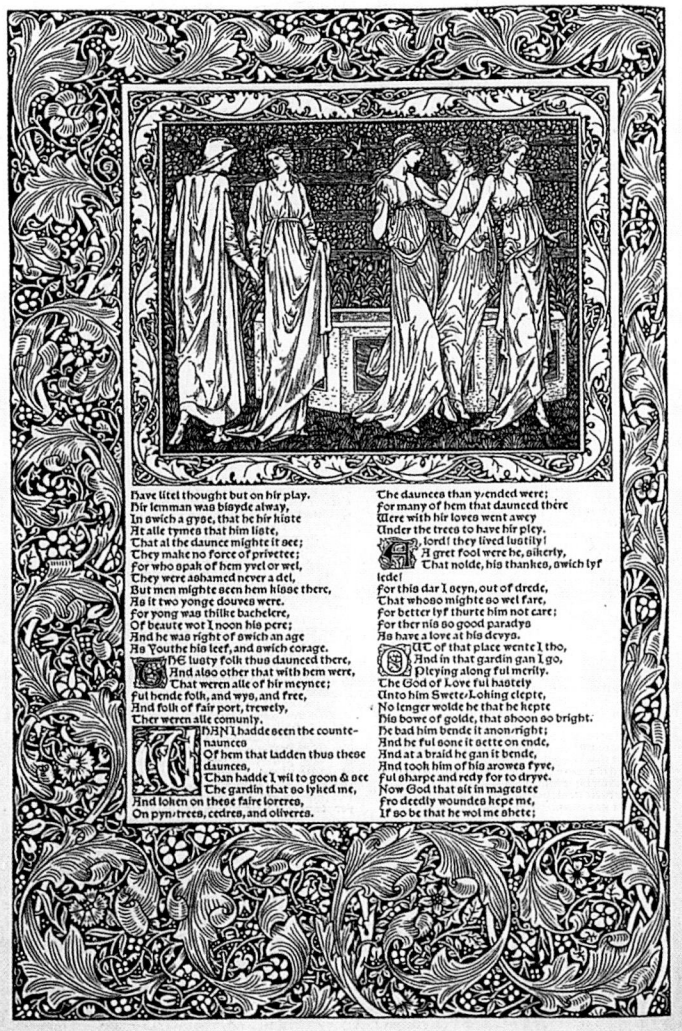

print runs and his own poor health, Morris continued to work with characteristic energy and created a series of sumptuous and ornate books.

I began printing books with the hope of producing some which would have a definite claim to beauty, while at the same time they should be easy to read ... Fifteenth Century books ... were always beautiful by force of the mere typography, even without the added ornament ... it was the essence of my undertaking to produce books which it would be a pleasure to look upon as pieces of printing and arrangements of type.

As part of his commitment he designed two new typefaces which would truly represent his ideals of beauty and clarity. 'Golden' was modelled on fifteenth-century Venetian print and his Gothic font (with the two versions, 'Troy' and 'Chaucer') developed from an earlier German Gothic type. The craftsmanship involved in creating new

Pages from *The Kelmscott Chaucer*, 1896 (William Morris Gallery, London). The lifelong creative collaboration of Morris and Burne-Jones achieved its supreme moment with the publication of this fine, dramatic work. The richness of the decorations, the open typography, the delicacy of the illustrations all conspire to create a magnificent celebration of an author and an age which provided a constant inspiration to them both.

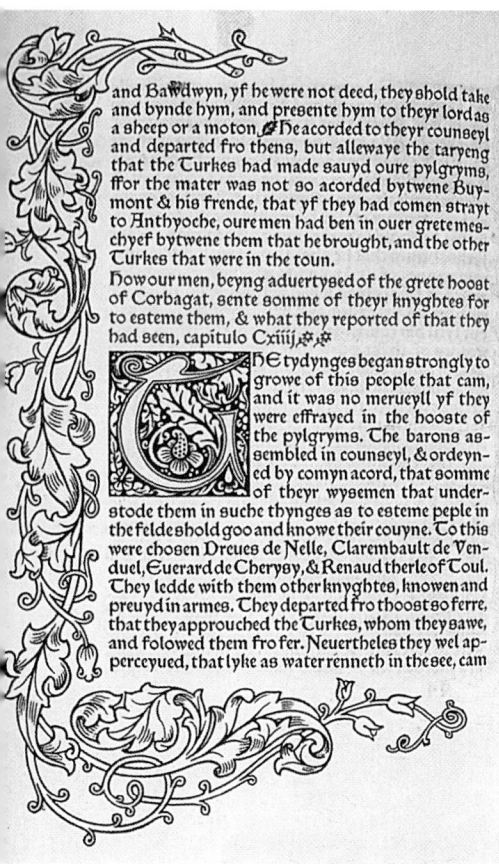

Page from *History of Godfrey of Boulogne* (Kelmscott Press, 1893). Morris chose classic texts to illustrate and decorate for the Kelmscott Press. Here the decorated border and capital letter are excellent examples of the techniques from illuminated manuscripts which Morris revived in modern printed form.

typefaces was as detailed and painstaking as the methods of dyeing or weaving. The decorative details, coloured inks, foliages and swirling natural designs flow through his decorated books in much the same way as through his printed fabrics.

The consummate achievement of the Press, indeed one of the most dazzling and impressive works of Morris's canon, is the Kelmscott Chaucer. It was a collaboration between Morris and Burne-Jones, the last in a lifelong friendship, dedication and artistic exchange. For them both it represented an attempt to relive the glories of Chaucer's ordered world and shape their own intimate, spiritual commitment to the ideals of that age, bearing it into a world of industrial wrong, of working slavery. Here was a truly liberated evocation of the spirit of man and nature, of decoration and beauty, of art and function. Although the very people for whom Morris fought in his lectures and street corner speeches could not hope to afford such an item it embodied its makers' holistic passion for order and justice. In 1893 they started work on the project, with Burne-Jones working on the illustrations, Morris on the borders and the decorated capital letters. A rich and powerful white leather-bound book it was like a medieval mare waiting for her knight, the reader, to engage; 425 copies were made for publication in 1894. It remains one of the most significant artistic works of the nineteenth century.

In the last five years of Morris's life the Kelmscott Press published over eighteen thousand copies across a total of fifty-three titles. All were meticulously hand printed with rigorous attention to detail and to every aspect of quality and design, forging a revival among the moribund state of printing and design at the time.

Cultural Legacy

William Morris died at Kelmscott Manor on 3 October 1896. In his last years he wrote further romances and poetry, continued to design tapestries and was revered by his Socialist companions, having reconciled with many of those who had rejected him from the Social Democratic Federation. He was a campaigner to the end, for social justice and artistic integrity and the intrinsic link between the two. His simple burial, in a plain oak coffin with wrought iron handles, was a fitting end for this honest conscientious man and his last words, 'I want to get the mumbo jumbo out of the world' sang through the philosophies and actions of his life, reaching far beyond the confines of his own generation. In the field of design and decorative art Morris provided a sense of purpose for designers showing them that they could help to make the world a better place, make art accessible to more than just those who could afford it and bring it to real people.

Morris's influence can be seen in the work of many of the great artists and art movements of the *fin de siècle* although none who followed could rival the breadth of his vision, his intricate weave of art and society, man and the natural world. His lectures on the honest place of decorative arts in the homes of real people inspired a sweep of young designers who gathered together to become the creative force of the Arts and Crafts Movement in the late 1880s. Arthur Mackmurdo started the Century Guild, a collection of interior designers, glass makers, brass workers, wrought iron and tile painters, on the basis of Morris's search for integrity in craft. C.F.A. Voysey's stylish, traditional work, Louis Comfort Tiffany's sweeping stained glasses, the lush wall-paper patterns of Lindsay Butterfield and Walter Crane for Liberty's of London, all found their spiritual origins in the principles which Morris embodied.

The Arts and Crafts Exhibition Society, which held its first exhibition in opposition to the formalism and elitism of the Royal Academy's summer shows, was greatly responsible for the inculcation of Morris's ideas in the next generation of designers. Other craftsmen like William de Morgan and Ernest Gimson (a furniture manufacturer) became part of the wave of interest in the return to first principles which Morris advocated so stridently. The impact of his appeal was not the originality of his work but its brilliant timelessness. His return to fifteenth-century art was not simply to find what was once good but to develop it further from the point where it was, in his analysis, corrupted by the

Bedroom suite, 1917, by C.R. Mackintosh (Victoria & Albert Museum, London). The suite of furniture, in mahogany and mother-of-pearl, shows Mackintosh as a fine craftsman, working to the same principles as Morris but extending them to his own use. The lofty elegance of his designs appears in all his pieces and conveys a careful sense of interior unity.

grandiose elitism of the Renaissance. He did not entirely approve of the Arts and Crafts Movement because it did not aim to address the root causes of the vulgar, showy art which it determined to undermine, but Morris's own philosophical and artistic work, however, enabled others to see and follow the brilliance of what he achieved without prescribing to its origins.

Tiffany and Gustav Stickly, major figures in the North American Arts and Crafts Movement, were heavily influenced by Morris's lectures and ideas, and looked forward to the total decorative schemes of Frank Lloyd Wright and his version of Morris's open, integrated approach to design. In Europe, Morris's care, craftsmanship and high standards were particularly emulated in textile design and book production. In Germany he was a primary influence in Walter Gropius's work and through him the Bauhaus school of design in the 1920s and 1930s. Although Morris's decorative schemes were found in the wealthy middle-class family homes of Holland Park in London, in Oxford and in large country houses in Staffordshire and Wiltshire, their depth and adaptability later influenced the decoration of the smaller houses in which most people now live. Morris's cultural impact extends to Oscar Wilde and the Aesthetic Movement whose 'art for art's sake' philosophy (another which did not gain Morris's approval) derived from Walter Pater's interpretation of Morris's declaration: 'To burn always with this bright and gem-like flame, to maintain this ecstasy is success in life ... for art comes to you professing frankly to give nothing but the highest quality to your moments as they pass, and simply for the moment's sake.'

Morris's vision was cast decisively beyond simple statements of aesthetics, it was born out of the energetic sense of commitment to justice and society which ignited his art. Progress was meaningless unless it improved the lives of man; the industrial madness of the Victorian age merely improved the lives of some at the expense of a mass of unskilled and unvalued humanity. His upbringing and the freedoms released by his wealth contrasted starkly with the nature of his conviction. This contradiction sparked the creative tension which still echoes in the timeless impact of his designs. 'Morris is not dead,' said his friends in the Social Democratic Foundation on his death, '... he lives in the heart of all true men and women still and will do so until the end of time.' Indeed many of his concerns, which are at the foundations of his burgeoning, lyrical designs in all their forms, are as relevant today as they were at the end of the nineteenth century.

Forget six counties overhung with smoke,
Forget the snorting steam and piston stroke,
Forget the spreading of the hideous town;
Think rather of the pack-horse on the down,
And dream of London, small, and white, and clean,
The clear Thames bordered by its gardens green.
The Earthly Paradise, *1868-70*

Dado, by Walter Crane, *c.* 1890
(Victoria & Albert Museum, London). Crane's wallpaper designs were exceptionally popular in the latter part of the nineteenth century. Like Morris he drew much of his inspiration from the natural world, although he used fewer decorative devices.

INDEX

William Morris. Strawberry Thief, 1883
(Victoria & Albert Museum, London)

William Morris. La Belle Iseult, 1858
(Tate Gallery, London)

William Morris. Design for Honeysuckle fabric, 1874
(Birmingham City Museum)

Dante Gabriel Rossetti. Blanzifiore (Snowdrops), 1873
(Private Collection)

Edward Burne-Jones. Minstrel, 1882-4
(Victoria & Albert Museum, London)

William Morris. Woodpecker, 1885
(William Morris Gallery, London)

When Adam delved and Eve span
Who was then the gentleman

Edward Burne-Jones. A Dream of John Bull, by William Morris
(Kelmscott Press, 1892)

Wandle, 1884.
(Victoria & Albert Museum, London)